THE WHOLE ART OF
VENTRILOQUISM

D1569372

ARTHUR PRINCE.

THE WHOLE ART
OF
VENTRILOQUISM

By
ARTHUR PRINCE

Second Edition
˙ (Revised)

Copyrighted in all Countries

WILL   GOLDSTON   LIMITED
LONDON, W.C.2, ENGLAND

Geo. Stevens & Co., Ltd., London.

Contents

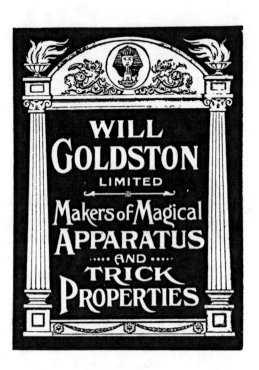

Introduction

By WILL GOLDSTON

WHEN I wrote the introduction to the first edition of " The Whole Art of Ventriloquism," I was confident ventriloquists throughout the world would be eager to read a work from the pen of the greatest ventriloquist in our time, I was right. The entire large edition was soon exhausted. Second-hand copies brought high prices. The demand for copies reach Will Goldston Limited daily from all countries, the demand must be satisfied and at a lower price than the previous edition. This is made possible since the printing blocks of the diagrams, a most costly part of book production does not enter into the costs of this edition.

Good wine needs no bush. And, similarly, Arthur Prince needs no commendation from me. The public who know him and his great achievements in the ventriloquial art will buy this book of his, with or without a foreword from my pen. Yet it may interest some to read the impressions I have formed of Arthur Prince and his work during my long friendship with him. Besides, I have a keen interest in his book, for it was I who persuaded him to write it. Every man, it is said, has within him the material for one good book. I realized that Arthur Prince had within him the material, not simply for a good book on ventriloquism, but for a veritable masterpiece on the subject. And so I induced him, busy man though he is, to burn the midnight oil and join the fellowship of authors.

Many years ago I first witnessed a ventriloquial performance by Arthur Prince. I
was visiting Dublin and noticed his name in
the the bill at the Empire there. He was
not then the great popular favourite that he
is now; but I had heard him mentioned as
one of the " coming men," and I decided to
see his performance. It was a revelation to
me of the possibilities of ventriloquism. So
far as I was concerned, " he came; he saw;
and he conquered." From beginning to end
his performance was a sheer delight to me.
So much so that, in order to see it again and
study its finer points, I visited the Empire
twice more that week.

On the following Sunday business affairs
necessitated my going from Dublin to
Belfast. By what I have always regarded
as good luck, Arthur Prince had to make
the same journey, and we had chosen the
same train. While we were awaiting it, I
saw him on the platform and introduced
myself to him. I told him how much I had
enjoyed his entertainment and asked per-
mission to have a talk with him about it and
his career generally. I suppose I risked a
snub, and from some public performers
doubtless I should have got one. But, being
a very courteous gentleman, Arthur Prince
received me most cordially, and when he
found that we were both going to Belfast,
suggested that we should travel together.

With that journey our friendship began.
At first our conversation was devoted to
ventriloquism. I knew enough of it to listen
intelligently and to prompt with occasional
remarks. But, in effect, " I sat at the feet
of Gamaliel." Afterwards, however, we

found that we had many interests in common; and the conversation became general, and we parted with mutual promises of other meetings and other talks.

There have been many such meetings and talks. I look back on them all with keen pleasure. Arthur Prince is a man of wide culture, with rare gifts of humour and effective conversation. Much have I learned from him; much joyous entertainment has he given me; for much—very much—am I the cheerful debtor of his friendship. An hour in his company is one to be recorded with a red letter.

What has Arthur Prince done for ventriloquism ? Ask rather what has he not done for it ? When he began his work ventriloquism was a comic opera sort of thing. It was almost entirely an affair of "make believe." The average ventriloquial entertainer knew little of the art, and substituted effrontery for skill. In his entertainment he used half a dozen or more figures. The figures spoke; but the voice was always that of the performer, and always it came, without effective disguise, from the selfsame place—the mouth of the performer. The change of voice to suit the character, the actual "throw" of the voice, in fact, all the verisimilitudes of the art, were absent.

I was nearly forgetting the trick ventriloquist. His figures **did** speak with different voices, and the voices **did** come from the figures themselves. But the effects were not obtained by ventriloquism. The figures were all of large size, and boys and girls, sometimes even men and women, were concealed within them. They did the talking; the performer only pretended to be a ventriloquist. Nowadays such a fraud seems almost incredible. Yet quite recently I witnessed a revival of it at a hall in a certain provincial town. The performer was a relic of the old school; his figures belonged to that school; his methods were its methods. As I watched him I felt that he ought to have been in a museum instead of on a public platform.

How different are the methods of Arthur Prince ! He has developed the art of ventriloquism to an extent hitherto unknown. His effects are all genuine products of that art. He obtains them with ease, but he does so only as the result of years of study and work. So far as ventriloquism is concerned, he is a self-taught man. His methods are his own. He has discovered new principles in the art, and has worked them out with infinite pains and applied them with rare success. In every department of ventriloquism he has effected improvements. Take, for instance, the matter of figure construction. Before the time of Arthur Prince ventriloquial figures were clumsily made and badly dressed. They were in no sense lifelike—rude caricatures of the human form divine. He has changed all that. His figures are perfectly modelled; they are " the real thing." Several times I have heard members of his audiences hazard the opinion that Arthur Prince was working with real persons and not dummies.

The best tribute to the methods of Arthur Prince is to be found in the fact that they have been imitated by so many other performers. I referred just now to the old school of ventriloquism. The new school owes its being to Arthur Prince. He created it, and has inspired it at every stage of its growth. Other ventriloquists speak of him as the Master Ventriloquist. They know what they owe to him, they know what he has done for them and the art they share with him.

I must not stand much longer between this book and its readers, but before concluding my appreciation of Arthur Prince I feel impelled to write a few words about his personality. From what I have already written it will be gathered that he is one of the best of good fellows. Certainly I have never known a better. He is also one of the best of good citizens. He takes an active interest in the welfare of all classes of the community. He is a generous supporter of charities, both by pecuniary gifts and by his performances. An all-round man: a credit to his country and to his profession.

I have finished. Here is the Master Book on Ventriloquism written by the Master Ventriloquist. May it receive all the attention it deserves.

CHAPTER I.

HOW DO YOU DO IT ?

I have been asked the question with which I head this chapter very many times. My invariable reply has been what the novelists call an "inscrutable smile." But now I am going to be much more communicative. Indeed, I am not only going to explain how I do it, but how my readers may do it as well.

My friend Will Goldston has said some very nice things in his introduction to this book about myself and my position in the ventriloquial world. So nice, that I blush as I read them ! Mr. Goldston is right in claiming that he induced me to write the book. May his claim that it will be a masterpiece on the subject of which it treats also prove right !

Ventriloquism, in the language of the dictionary, is the act or art of speaking in such a manner as to cause the hearers to believe that the sound comes, not from the person speaking, but from a different source. The name originated from the erroneous supposition that the sounds uttered were formed in the belly, whereas they are formed by the same organs as the emissions of sound commonly, viz., the larynx, the palate, the tongue, the lips, etc., only that to increase the illusion the performer moves the lips as little as possible. The art of ventriloquism depends mainly on two things : (1) the power of appreciating the value of sounds at certain given distances or when hindered by obstacles; and (2) the power of imitating or reproducing the diminished value of such sounds. Thus to represent a man speaking outside a window, the ventriloquist should know exactly the value of such sounds inside a room if actually produced outside, and also be able to reproduce them by accurate imitation.

But how to do it ? Well, I have tried to explain this exhaustively in the following pages. I have entitled my book **The Whole Art of Ventriloquism,** and I have endeavoured to realize the title. The subject seems to me to group itself conveniently into three parts, and I have adopted this grouping. The first part relates to the mechanism of ventriloquial voice, and describes the principles on which the art of ventriloquism is based and the correct methods of applying these principles. The second part is devoted to imitations of animals, birds and musical instruments. Such imitations, ventriloquially interpreted, are very popular with audiences. The third part deals with ventriloquial entertainments with figures. It contains information as to the construction of figures, mechanical appliances for working them, and suitable dialogues between them and the performer.

A word of warning to the beginner. Do not expect to be able to duplicate all the feats of that famous fictional hero Valentine Vox. The book which bears his name as its title is most entertaining. But the ventriloquial parts are greatly exaggerated. The author of the book knew something about ventriloquism; but he wrote from his imagination rather than his knowledge. For instance, he constantly makes Valentine Vox throw his voice to impossible places, having no regard to the situation of the different characters at the time of the incident. For actual practice the performer must stand between the listener and the " supposed place " of the voice, and should name the place before throwing the voice. The author of **Valentine Vox** did not trouble about this. Still, the book has been of use to practical ventriloquists. Mr. McCabe, for instance, read it to effect. So I have reason to suspect did Lieutenant Cole.

I am desirous that all readers of **The Whole Art of Ventriloquism** should achieve ventriloquial success. I advise careful study and constant practice. Some students are slow to learn, others make progress more rapidly. If you love the art of ventriloquism make up your mind to be successful —and you will be delighted with the progress you will make.

Part I.

PREFACE.

I have already defined this part as describing the principles on which the art of ventriloquism is based and the correct methods of applying those principles. It should be studied by the reader again and again, for a complete understanding of it is necessary to full success in the art. As far as possible I have avoided technical expressions and endeavoured to use ordinary language. I think that, with the help of the accompanying diagrams, every explanation will soon be grasped. Here and there it may seem to some of my readers that I have entered into detail somewhat too fully and exactly. I plead not guilty. It is impossible to be too full or too exact when one is laying the groundwork of an art. I hope that this book will produce many successful ventriloquists, and I intend that their success shall be based on the surest and most thorough groundwork possible.

CHAPTER II.

On the opposite page is a diagram showing the human vocal organs. I wish my readers to study with particular care the palate and palatine arch or sounding board (E and F in the diagram) and also the dental arch, as they are the most important organs from the point of view of ventriloquism. The larynx (H) causes the protuberance in the throat known as the Adam's apple.

The vocal chords or lips will be found just underneath (I). The false vocal chords are marked **4**.

The rest of the figures should also be studied, for everything shown in the diagram has some degree of importance. Where in the following pages I refer to any of the figures or letters the reader should consult the diagram.

Sound.—Sound (including that of the voice) is produced by vibrations of a solid body, or by the undulations of a fluid. Note the bellows, lungs (L), bronchial tubes (M), trachea (K), and the windpipe, which by creating a current of air acts as a motive power and causes the vibrations.

The vocal lips, double like the reeds of the oboe, and the larynx with its neighbouring cavities, form the resounding body. To prolong the voice sound, one must economise air by controlling the function of expiration. Controlling expiration constitutes what is called FIXING THE VOICE.

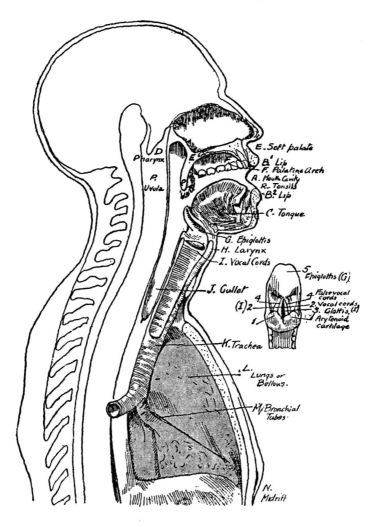

E. Soft palate
B¹ Lip
F. Palatine Arch
A. Mouth Cavity
R. Tonsils
B² Lip
C. Tongue
D Pharynx
E
P. Uvula
G. Epiglottis
H. Larynx
I. Vocal Cords
J. Gullet
5 Epiglottis (G)
4. False vocal cords
(I) 2 — 2. Vocal cords
1 — 3. Glottis (I)
Arytenoid cartilage
K. Trachea
L. Lungs or Bellows.
M. Bronchial Tubes
N. Midriff

Breathing.—We know what the sound is, and how it is caused. Obviously before we can send out air (expiration) we must learn how to take it in (inspiration).

The principle of **correct breathing** is the foundation of the art of ventriloquism, and needs great attention. Deep breathing is of the utmost importance for bringing the fresh air into the lungs, and for developing the chest cavity, but it must be done carefully, and not overdone, as in that case it is liable to strain the heart, or cause a chronically enlarged chest (known in medical phraseology as emphysema), or to pre-dispose one to bronchitis. Diaphragmatic breathing is the correct way to breathe, as the air fills the whole of the lungs even to the back and lower parts.

The following hints for breathing exercises are based upon knowledge gained by years of practice. I therefore give them with authority : —

(1) On rising in the morning stand by the open window (or in the open air), place the right foot forward, and the hands raised as in figure. Then inhale slowly through the nose (the weight of the body must be on the right foot during the inspiration). After inhaling as much air as the lungs will take, hold it for as many seconds as you comfortably can. Then bring the weight back on to the left foot, dropping the hands to your sides limply, and slowly exhale.

Repeat movement, changing the feet, and do every movement slowly.

(2) Place the feet ten inches apart. Rest the hands on the hips. Force the head back and inhale slowly, taking care not to move the shoulders. Get the air into the lower part of the lungs (diaphragm). Having taken in as much air as you can, bend the body forward and say in a prolonged way, " Thanks." This gets all the stale air out of the lungs. Wait for two seconds (one— two) and commence over again.

These exercises should be done for ten minutes every morning, and should be repeated frequently during the day.

CHAPTER III.

Mouth and Teeth.—General good health is an important matter to the ventriloquist. His mouth and teeth must be in perfect condition.

The health of the mouth and throat I believe to be the secret of general good health and the whole body, and the feeling of well being which is so essential to a public entertainer.

The ventriloquist particularly must have not only his full complement of teeth, but they and the tissues around the mouth must be free from infection from the myriads cf germs which nearly all mouths contain.

In this way the throat and bronchial tubes are protected, and one goes the year round free and immune from colds and coughs.

The teeth and the spaces between them present an area of a great number of square inches for bacterial growth.   If the teeth are kept clean, i.e., absolutely or surgically clean, they will not decay, and a great point is scored.

More important than decay of the teeth is inflammation around them, so prevalent amongst all classes of people in this age of soft and highly fermentable food.   This inflammation leads to what is called pyorrhœa, which is now known to be such a dangerous disease, both by causing the loss of the teeth and by predisposing the body to other diseases.

Now the throat, with the tonsils guarding it, is another bugbear, as waste and poisonous products from the mouth are absorbed here and cause general indisposition, sore throat, laryngitis, fever and a host of troubles.   If, on the other hand, poisonous products from the mouth are swallowed, they give rise to indigestion, anæmia, and general ill-health of the body.

Every one should have his mouth and throat examined at least once every three months by a surgeon skilled in this line of work, great care being taken that he is a registered practitioner, as so many mouths are ruined by advertising " sharks " calling themselves experts.   Properly qualified men do not advertise, and usually exhibit a small brass plate only with their name on it, their practice growing simply by recommendation.

For some years I have followed a routine which has given every satisfaction and is essentially as follows: —

As regards the teeth.—The most important time to brush the teeth is the last thing at night just before retiring; brushing in the morning and after meals is useful, **but last thing at night is essential.** This should be done with a brush with unbleached bristles. This brush is of medium size with very stiff bristles, and is so designed that it will get to all parts of the mouth, and the bristles are so arranged that they can be forced in between the teeth, where decay and pyorrhœa usually start. The brushing should be done with rotating movement of the wrist, brushing the lower teeth upwards and the uppers downwards, at the same time brushing the gums hard against the teeth.

This daily brushing of the gums takes the place of the hard, fibrous diet which our ancestors used, and which kept their mouths healthy and the teeth free from decay. If the gums bleed it is a sign that they need the brushing more vigorously than usual.

Two brushes should be in commission, to be used alternately, so that one is always dry and stiff; after use they should be hung up to dry in the sun.

A powder should be used once a day (at night); it is so much more effective than a paste, which gives the sensation of cleanliness but which is not so efficacious.

After brushing the teeth the mouth should be rinsed with water (cold is best), to which a few drops of a good mouthwash is added.

The throat may be gargled at the same time with the same solution.   There are many good mouth washes and tooth powders on the market; personally, I have these made up for me from the prescription of a distinguished specialist, to whom I am greatly indebted for the continued health of my teeth and jaws.

The Nose.—For the purpose of cleanliness and to obtain clearness of voice it is necessary that the nose be douched occasionally. This should be done in the following manner—

One teaspoonful of salt should be added to a pint of water which has been boiled. Then, while one is breathing through the mouth, this solution should be allowed to run up one nostril.   By tilting the head it will run down the other nostril. Convenient and cheap nasal douches can be obtained at any drug store. The important point is to breathe through the mouth forcibly during the operation, and to use a mild saline solution.   The solution should be warm, but not hot, and should be freshly prepared on each occasion.

Jaw Exercise.—Close lips tightly. Drop lower jaw without parting lips. Move lower jaw from side to side, forward and backward. Now open the mouth wide and then close firmly. Do this several times, as all the facial muscles should be exercised. The control of these muscles is the most difficult part of the work of voice illusion. I have found these exercises invaluable to me in obtaining such control.

Throat and Neck Exercises.—Hold head up, looking at your own height. Stretch the neck as high as you can; then relax. Now stiffen the neck and press backwards as though forcing a weight away with the back of the head, drawing chin well in (see Figures on next page). Then relax. Do this several times in succession it strengthens the neck muscles.

Tongue Exercise.—Raise the tongue towards the roof of the mouth without touching the palatine arch. Then bring it down quickly to the lower jaw until a " click " sound is produced, just like a hammer striking a xylophone. Notes can be breathed on the tongue, and after a little practice the perfect imitation of the above instrument is obtained, though not loud enough for stage use. (see Part II of this book). In beginning the tongue exercises the lips should be slightly parted and then firmly closed. This will give the necessary flexibility to the tongue.

Rubbing.—The muscles of the throat, nose, and jaws require rubbing firmly daily. This keeps the blood in good circulation and freshens these parts. The whole of the body should be rubbed or massaged daily. I can recommend Müller's **My System** (obtainable at all bookstalls). It should be consulted as to this. I have found it most useful.

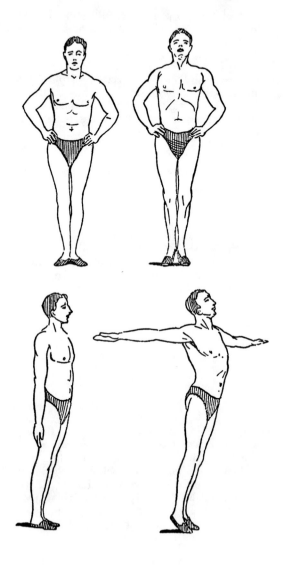

CHAPTER IV.

My book is not intended as a guide to health, but at the same time I would say that health is a most important factor in obtaining success as a ventriloquist. Neglect of the teeth, eyes, nose, ears, or throat is a fatal mistake for the student of ventriloquism to make.

Health is in a way the foundation of all real success—certainly of success in ventriloquism. It has been asserted that ventriloquists are short-lived. That is not so, except in the case of those who do not keep fit. To keep fit, lead a healthy life, get plenty of open-air exercise, play games, mix with people healthy in mind and body, and look upon all your work and practice as a hobby, not slavery. The foundation is thus laid.

Head and Voice Exercise.—Place the lips together and hum the notes from middle C

to G. Then gradually get half a note higher, and so on. Hum easily and without strain. On opening the mouth and doing the same exercise you will find you cannot go so high at first. With a little practice you will overcome this difficulty. If you force yourself, you may be able to get one or two notes higher; but I strongly advise you not to do so, as this is the falsetto voice, and the strain so produced injures the vocal chords. Now do the following exercises: —

Hum with closed lips and half-closed throat. Now gradually open mouth, keeping throat closed. You thus have the female voice. These sounds are placed at the back of the front teeth. The different sounds, notes or noises, are brought about by the opening and closing of the throat, pressure on the vocal chords, and flexibility of the tongue. The tongue and palate are the two principal organs for producing sound. Here is an example: Open the throat and say, " There you are "; you will notice how gruff the voice is. Now half close the throat and speak the same sentence at the back of the teeth. You get an entirely different sound. Now do the same thing again, gradually opening and closing the throat. You will find this an excellent exercise for giving flexibility to the tongue, throat, and vocal chords, and you will shortly find you have the " mimic " voice.

Chest Voice.—The chest voice is produced from your natural voice, the throat being open. The vowels O, A, E, will give you the round note. Practise those three vowels, throwing the head back, on the following scale.

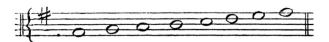

On rising in the morning, cough and then cry, " Hullo—o—o ! " You will find this will awaken the vocal chords. Do not shout too loud and above all do not strain.

Head to Chest Voice Exercises.—Oo—Ah —Oo—Ah—o—a—h— on the following

notes. This exercise is to transmit the voice from head to chest.

Humming and the Female Voice.—The humming of different notes not in your natural voice but in the head voice (falsetto) constantly, will be good exercise for the " female " voice. The humming is placed at the back of the soft **palate** (E) and **pharynx** (D) see diagram. In a very short while you will be able to say short sentences and with a little imagination you will be able to imitate the different female voices. The following are some notes as to the personation of woman characters : —

The Woman Pedlar *The Coster Girl* *The Laundry Woman* *The Char Woman, etc.*	Speak in a loud harsh voice, without any thought of grammar.
The Bazaar Lady *The Duchess* *The Would-be Society Lady and all educated Women*	Close the pharynx. This is done by allowing no air to pass through or out of the nose. Speak in a slow, modulated voice, precise, and very correctly as though you were bored.
The Flapper *The Lady in Love* *The Seaside Girl* *The School Girl* *The Sporting Girl*	Speak rather quickly, and clip the words sharply at the end. The school girl giggles. The love-lorn lady talks in a dreamy way. The sporting girl's voice is crisp, sharp and she talks only of sport.

The high thin pitch of the child voice is easily acquired after you have mastered the falsetto voice.

Great care must be exercised not to strain the vocal chords; directly the voice gets tired, rest.

A little playlet will be found in Part III of this book, giving an idea of the appropriate dialogue for the above characters.

Gruntings and the Male Voice.

The Colonel.—" Halt! Shun!'' All words used by the Colonel are sharp with "clip" after the words.

Sergeant Major.—The Sergeant Major the same.

Naval Captain.—The Naval Captain is more round and "no clip." This is the "Growl voice," and is produced at the back of the throat (see 2 and A).

The Parson.—This "voice" is very easy to do. At the end of sentences the voice should be raised slightly. At the end of the words should be pronounced "ar." "You don't mean to tell me "; "you surprise me," etc.

The Coster. The real Coster's voice is quite plaintive (except the brutal kind, of course). Speak "low (not softly), omit the H from words commencing with that letter (see Sketch in Part III).

The Englishman. Lazy of voice, very precise, very quiet, rather gruff at times, quietly dominating, always a " weighing you up " look about your eyes, a slow thinker except in action.

The Scotchman. " Is that so ? Perhaps you're right," as though always questioning our statement. Be very careful and precise in speaking, bold, fearless, and dignified.

The Irishman. Be bright, buoyant, make light of troubles, poetic, musical, humorous, pathetic; change into the different moods quickly.   The whole face smiles, yet behind it there is bold action.

American, French and German impressions are given in Part III.

CHAPTER V.

The Far-distant Voice.—Distant ventriloquism imposes a slight strain on the voice; so I advise the student who combines the " near " and " far " voice in his entertainment to leave the " far " voice until the last.   The " far " voice is produced by forcing sound from a very tightly closed throat, in this way:—

Close your lips tightly.   Now close the throat and roll the back part of the tongue to the diaphragm and gradually open the mouth.   You have the buzzing sound of a bee or wasp when flying.   The closed lips give a very distant sound and the open lips a nearer sound.   The greater the pressure of air forced through the tightly closed throat, the louder the sound.   Practise this steadily until you have obtained the perfect " Bee Imitation," and then you have the voice-throwing foundation.

Should the blood rush to the head whilst practising this, bend the body from the knees and try and sit on your heels.   Place hands on hips, rise on toes, then holding body erect and, looking at your own height, sink the pelvis to the heels.   Then straighten up and repeat until the head is quite clear.

After having thoroughly mastered the " Bee Imitation," you proceed to practise the vowels:—

Say in your natural voice, " A, E, I, O, U," and repeat same in the " far " voice. Do this in sing-song tones. This is good practice for " Echo Imitation." Then say in natural voice, " Hullo ! " and repeat in the " far " voice " 'Ullo ! 'Ullo ! " (The letter H cannot be sounded in the " far " voice).

NATURAL VOICE.—I say, Tom.

FAR VOICE.—What do you want ?

NATURAL VOICE.—Breakfast is ready.

FAR VOICE.—All right, I'll be with you in a minute, etc., etc.

It is not necessary to move the lips for the " far " voice. At the time of writing I am doing the above myself without any lip movement. At first you may find some difficulty in keeping the lips still, but you can rectify that later. Keep up the " Bee Imitation " by placing the sound in the same place. Then say " 'Ullo! 'Ullo!" and as only a little air comes through the throat the voice away will sound a long way off. Keep the " 'Ullo!" practice up until you think you can add other words.

Pronouncing Words.—Some writers on ventriloquism state that it is impossible to pronounce certain letters. I disagree with them. If the student follows my instructions closely, he will find he can pronounce each and every letter. The difficult letters are B, M, N, P, and W.

c

It is quite unnecessary to say " Gred and gutter " for " Bread and Butter," or " Kritty Kolly " for " Pretty Polly," or " 'ice, 'ice," for " Nice, nice." Bread is pronounced " brr'ead " with a slight roll of the " r " not beread." The above letters are pronounced by the ventriloquist with the breath, tongue, and dental dome. Any word commencing with " B " must be pronounced slowly, taking care to allow the breath to roll over the tongue. Pronounce the next letter forcibly and slowly.

The same rule exists with regard to the letter " P," only a little more air is used over the tongue, the tip of which is behind the lower teeth.

M and N are pronounced sharply. W is pronounced slowly and the syllables precisely, " Do-ble-u." A good exercise is to say the letters after each other, with yourself as the critic.

The other letters of the alphabet afford good practice for these difficult ones. Make up your mind to overcome this so-called impossibility of pronouncing B, M, N, P, and W.

CHAPTER VI.

The Ventriloquist without the Figure.

Quite a number of entertainments can be given by a ventriloquist without the aid of a " Figure." Here are a few from my own repertoire : —

Friends Outside the Window.

The ventriloquist approaches the window, holds the curtain slightly apart, and listens. (This draws the attention of the audience to the outside of the window). Two men are supposed to be returning from work and stop to greet each other. (The " far " voice is used and the throat is tightly closed for one voice and slightly closed for the other).

No. 1.—'Ullo! 'Arry, 'ow are yer? I'm glad to see yer.

No. 2.—I'm all right, Bill. Did you see Joe yesterday?

No. 1.—Yus! he's got two lovely black eyes! Who decorated 'em?

No. 2.—'Is ole woman. She's a gasbag, you know; Joe says they ought to be chucked in the river.

No. 1.—So she dotted him one.

No. 2.—Not one—six—and with the rolling pin.

No. 1.—Ain't you glad you're not married?

No. 2.—You bet I am. Well, good-night, Bill.

No. 1.—Good-night, 'Arry.

At the end the ventriloquist drops the curtain.

The Returning Roysterer and the Policeman.

Singing heard in the distance (latest music-hall song). Ventriloquist goes to the window, pulls curtain aside, and listens.

The reveller stops singing and talks to a policeman.

REVELLER. 'Ullo! Mr. Bluebird, 'ow are yer?

POLICEMAN. Go along there. Get out of it.

REVELLER. All right, you are unso'ble (singing heard and dies away in the distance).

The ventriloquist now opens window and speaks to the policeman. The throat is loosened here, as the window is open and the voice must be heard louder. But do not speak louder.

VENTRILOQUIST. Do you have many like that about here?

POLICEMAN. No ! sir, he's been to a meeting.

VENTRILOQUIST. Of his club, I suppose.

POLICEMAN. No, Trades Union.

VENTRILOQUIST. Whisky Trade?

POLICEMAN. Yes, sir.

VENTRILOQUIST. Good-night, constable.

Ventriloquist closes the window and pulls the curtains to. As he does so the singing fades away.

I count the above one of the finest bits of " far " voice work I do.

The Sleeping Child.

Ventriloquist opens the door, or has screen which is supposed to mask floor. (The child voice is used in this intonation).

VENTRILOQUIST. Are you asleep, Jimmie?

CHILD. Yes, daddy.

VENTRILOQUIST. I thought you were.

CHILD. Well, my eyes are closed.

VENTRILOQUIST. All right. (Pause).

CHILD. Daddy!

VENTRILOQUIST. Yes, dear.

CHILD. Who killed Cock Robin?

VENTRILOQUIST. I don't know, dear.

CHILD. Who is the lady who kisses me and tells me to be a good boy?

VENTRILOQUIST (dropping paper on floor and smiling at door). That is your mother, dear.

CHILD. Oh! did she kill Cock Robin?

VENTRILOQUIST (petulantly). No dear! Go to sleep. (Pause).

CHILD. Daddy!

VENTRILOQUIST. Yes, dear, what is it now?

CHILD. I wish you'd find out who killed Cock Robin for me.

VENTRILOQUIST. I will to-morrow.

CHILD. Daddy!

VENTRILOQUIST. Yes, dear.

CHILD. Where is the lady now?

VENTRILOQUIST. She has to attend her meeting, dear.

CHILD. What meeting?

VENTRILOQUIST. Suffrage meeting.

CHILD. What's that?

VENTRILOQUIST. I don't know, dear.

CHILD. Me no like suffrage people.

VENTRILOQUIST.   Say your prayers and go to sleep.

CHILD.   God bless daddy.   God bless Teddie Bear, and poor little Cock Robin. Amen!

VENTRILOQUIST.   God bless mother.

CHILD.   God bless the lady who sleeps in our house (sometimes).

Ventriloquist rises after a pause, and says softly, " Are you asleep ? "   Getting no answer, he slowly moves away and child calls out—

CHILD.   Good-night, daddy.

VENTRILOQUIST.   Good-night, dear.

A Distinct Novelty

An Eight-day Clock changes instantly into
a Ventriloquial Knee Figure

Part II.

PREFACE.

In writing this part of my book I have assumed that before studying it the reader will have acquired a knowledge of the general principles of the ventriloquial art as expounded in my previous part. Accordingly I have made the explanations of the various " imitation " effects as brief and direct as possible. But in working them out for himself the reader must apply those general principles. He must also study the originals of the various suggested imitations. Success in this form of ventriloquism is partly an affair of " voices " and partly of " ear." Neglect neither aim at perfection in both.

CHAPTER VII.

The following are reliable methods for imitating the " speech " of certain animals—

Cow.—Form an " O " with the thumb and index finger of the left hand and cover the hand with the right. Hollow both palms through and put your mouth into the " O " made by the left hand, and then say or groan " Ooh-ah-ooh-ah." Open right hand as you say " Ah ! " and you have the exact imitation of a cow. The more " open " nasal sound you produce, the better result you obtain.

HANDS FOR COW

Donkey.—Draw in the breath at " He " and force out right from the throat at " Haw ! " " He-haw ! " "He-haw ! " " He-haw ! " Say " Haw ! Haw ! Haw ! " spasmodically and softer on the last two " Haws." Opening and closing of the throat gives different " cow " sounds. The Bull is the same as above, only louder.

Lion.—Groan or growl voice right from the throat. " E—ough! E-ough-ow-ow-ow!"

Dog.—Laugh " Ow! ow! ow!" short and sharp. Different barks of dogs are made by tightening and opening the throat.

Puppy.—Tightly close the throat and force the breath through with jerks until you acquire the " squeak " voice. This is used for both the puppy and the cat imitation (see that the throat is tightly closed and the tongue rolled at the back of the mouth).

Pig.—Grunt "Eugh! Eugh!" Short grunts and then long ones. For the squeal put the throat same as for the parakeet, then tighten it up, draw in the flexibility of the throat. Common sense will teach you the rest.

Horse.—Watch the horse and following sound can be easily acquired. The hardest part is the neighing. This is done by drawing in the breath sharply through the throat and the back will vibrate the correct sound. Say " E-e-e." Prolonged, sharp and gruff neighing is made by the tightening and loosening of the throat.

With practice and the use of his own powers of observation the student will be able to imitate other animals. The " seal " speech, for instance, is a sharp inward gasp through the open throat. A day at the Zoo, starting in the early morning and remaining until sunset, will give you all sorts of ideas. Practise on the animals themselves. If you can deceive them, you will deceive that " two-legged radish," man.

Birds are mostly imitated by whistling with the fingers and mouth. The " trills " of the birds are made by the tip of the tongue. I place the tips of my fingers into my mouth and grip them lightly with the teeth, breathing over the dental arch the different notes required. The tongue does the rest. Some bird mimics use their throat only. The flexibility of throat is wonderful in the case of some performers. The plaintive call of the wren, the blackbird, thrush, robin, etc., can be imitated once you have got the note (by practice) by watching and listening. Get out into the country or parks for a day, and when you hear a bird singing, track it down and see what bird it is. A book on birds in any library will furnish you with the different plumage of birds.

Cock-Crowing.—This is done by the drawing the breath inward and trying to say " Oo-o-oodle oo." (Try and say "Cock-a-doodle-doo"). You must be very precise and pick each syllable out sharply.

Hen Chuckling.—This is made through or by the top back of the throat, "Uck, uck, uck-er-ka." The last "dek-ka" is harder than the beginning of the syllable.

Little Chicks.—Whistle inward softly (with pressed-up lips) spasmodically.

Parrot.—With the throat not too tightly closed, force a growl through and then say in a high key, "Allo, pretty Polly, Ullo, Sarah, it's time, Polly! Polly!" The " P " is pronounced softly. Make a slight pause between the words and lower voice at end of words.

There are one or two other birds you can imitate, using the above methods, such as the crow (say " Caw-caw "). The squeak of the parakeet is used by holding the throat in the same position as for the parrot imitation. Draw in the breath sharply and say, " E-e-e," with the guttural sound.

CHAPTER VIII.

The following are the methods for imitating certain well-known musical instruments—

Trombone.—This imitation is very simple. Teeth tightly closed. Now strongly force a hum through the teeth spasmodically, and at the end of some of the notes tighten the lips, and at the same time force a

TROMBONE

stronger hum through the teeth.   After very little practice you will find you have a very fine and loud imitation of the instrument.

Cornet.—Many books tell you this should not be attempted with the lips. I utterly disagree with them.   The difference between the trombone and the cornet is made by the teeth and lips.   In this imitation the teeth are parted and the lips firmly, not tightly closed. The notes are forced through the mouth.

CORNET

Saxaphone and Basso.—Teeth tightly closed. Fill the mouth with air, puff the cheeks, and the notes are breathed out from the

SAXAPHONE

back of the throat. Tongue raised in centre. The tip of the tongue is nearly always placed against the inside of the bottom teeth, and raised accordingly in the centre of the palate.

Clarionet.—Lips formed in the shape of an
" O," teeth apart, half fill the mouth
with air, sound the notes right from the
throat and say, "Tool-ee," "Tool-ee-tee"
(dental arch), the tip of the tongue break·
ing the word on the front of the palate.
Many other instruments can be imitated
by practice. " Teeth and tongue " work
is the all-important consideration.

CLARINETTE

Banjo.—For this, use the head voice.
Practice on ' pang " and " tang." For
the lower notes " Prang, tang-a-tang,
tang-a-tang, prang, prang, prang," etc.

One-String Fiddle.—" Grun " voice at back
of throat for the low notes and force the
notes up to the " head " voice for the
high notes. This imitation should be a
little nasal. Practise on the word
" Th-eh-eh."

Harp.—Fill the mouth with air, and say,
" Plim-plim, plim-plim, plim-plim." The
" head " voice is used and the remainder
of the effect is obtained by wagging the
tongue from side to side of the open
mouth.

Xylophone.—Put the open left hand (slightly arched) at the side of your mouth, breathe the notes, and hit the palm of your left hand with your right open hand.

Violoncello.—This is done by the " grunt " voice, lips closed.   The grunt voice (as you know), is produced at the back of the throat and the higher notes are forced to the top of the dental arch (head voice). Slur the notes with a pathetic drawl.

Other instruments can be imitated by listening to them.   The throat and resounding board should now be so flexible that the sound will place itself.

Whistling can also be brought into play for some instruments.

CHAPTER IX.

When doing imitations as in the previous chapters I used to find the following dialogue very useful : —
" How nice it is to get away from the noise and racket of a great city and migrate to the country to see the bright harmonious colouring of nature and enjoy the restfulness of it all.   Well, I stayed at a farm-house and when I got used to the nasty smell of my tiny bedroom I was all right.   Do you know why they keep the windows always shut?   No.   Well, I found it out, so I'll tell you.   It is because the various live stock of the farm commence to greet the morn about

4.30 a.m. First you hear that important member of the contingent, who has as many wives as feathers, start (cock-crow). He is the Lord High Muck-a-muck of the henwalk. Then comes the rest of his kind, who let him know he is not the only wife-owner in the world, and this goes on for half-an-hour (various cock-crows). Now this (hen chuckles). Then they wake up the ducks (duck quacking, cock-crowing, hen chuckling, ad lib.). Then the farmer knocks at your door and asks if you would like to see a bit of farm life. By this time you find it impossible to sleep and so out you go and nearly stumble over Mrs. Plymouth Rock, with her brood (chick imitation). You try and find Mr. Farmer, and the cows let you know it is milking time (cow imitation). Then the pigs call you (pig imitation). Then you hear the bull (bull imitation); now the calves (calf imitation), and, you find yourself amongst all the farm life. (Here imitate horse, cow, bull, chickens, pigeons, ducks, little chickens, pigs, birds, all in a rapid succession, and you have given a delightful and interesting entertainment lasting fifteen minutes or thereabouts.''

For an encore of this dialogue I would approach the conductor and ask him if he would allow his gentlemen of the orchestra to sound me a note or two upon their instruments. First, the cornet would give me a bar or two, which I would imitate. Then the trombone, bassoon, etc.

This was all rehearsed on the Monday with the orchestra, and the bars of the music were given in such a way that I could mimic them playing as softly as they could. I used to finish up with the following:—

D

" Have you ever heard this kind of thing when passing a public house?   One man keeping the door open with his foot and playing the cornet with one hand, and a very beercolic—1 mean bucolic—individual struggling with the trombone. (Imitation)."

Here are some other imitations—neither animal nor birds nor instrumental!

Fireworks.—Sky - rocket   and   catherine wheel.   These are easily imitated with the knowledge the student now possesses.   All that is required is to wait until November 5th, and then he can hear the sounds he wants to imitate free from some of his friends' displays.

The Gramophone.—Hold the nose with the thumb and index finger of the left hand, and form a funnel with the remaining three fingers and palm of the left hand. Complete the funnel with the right hand and make it as well as it possibly can be made by the hands like a gramophone funnel.   Have a little saliva at the back of the throat.   Having previously taken in a long breath, pinch the nose hard and the " growl " voice at the back of the throat forced on the top of the palate does the rest.   Of course you can move the lips. Great help can be obtained by listening to an instrument for half-an-hour.

Opening a Soda-Water Bottle.—Imagine the bottle in your left hand and the cork-screw in the right hand.   Now put the lower lip behind the top teeth, then force hard with the breath, until the lower lip is forced from behind the top teeth.   The tongue comes to the top of the palate, and completes the sound made like gas escaping from the bottle.

CORKSCREW

SODA WATER

Tyre Valve.—Same as above, only more force.

Bottles of Claret.—The sound of the corkscrew is made by the tongue being placed against the top teeth and a little air forced through. The sound of the cork leaving the bottle is made by closing the lips tightly and drawing in air sharply. Then open the lips quickly. (Or, put the second finger on the inside of the cheek and force it around until it comes out of the mouth with a " pop.") As you pour out the liquid the sound is given by hitting the bottom of the lower jaw with the lower part of the tongue.

Sawing Wood.—A little saliva is held on the centre of the tongue (the tip at the bottom of the teeth). Now draw the breath in and through the saliva and then expel it sharply. As you force the air out of your mouth raise the centre of the tongue to the dental arch. When going over a "knot" force the tongue nearer to the dental arch. It is a good idea to have a piece of board, nearly sawn through, with some sawdust on the top. At the end of the imitation you wipe the sawdust with your hand and give the board a knock which breaks it.

Circular Saw.—Purse the lips up together and blow the air out. Make the movement with your hands by placing the plank ready for sawing and pushing it along. Force out the air right from the lungs and up the open throat through the pursed-up lips. Tighten the lips occasionally to give the impression of the saw cutting through the " knots."

Bluebottle Fly.—Put the lips together and draw in the air through a small aperture at the side of the mouth. (See that the lips are dry). Chase the fly over the window pane and in the act of catching it open the lips wider and stop. The end of the imitation I leave to the imagination of the individual reader.

Part III.

PREFACE.

In my work as a ventriloquist I have specialized with the single figure. In every case I have endeavoured to make that figure a live character. I would advise my readers to do the same. Let your figures play distinct character parts in the sketches you present. Their personalities must be quite distinct from your own. And their dialogue must be uniformly consistent with their personalities. They must look and talk like human beings if you wish your audiences to accept them as such during your performances.

CHAPTER X.

Personality of your Figure or Figures.— Your figures should be dressed correctly, according to the characters they represent. Don't have an impossible or grotesque character. See that the face of the figure is properly moulded to look as human as possible, and keep it thoroughly clean.

Give " him " or " her " a name and a voice. Never use the words you have given to a figure, and never practise that voice unless it is with the figure. The " he " or " she " must have individuality. Some ventriloquists indulge in a number of " movements " such as raising the top lip, winking, spitting (a filthy and inartistic movement this), crying, wig-moving, etc. I advise my readers to use only natural movements (see explanation further in book). My " Jim," for instance, has only three levers: mouth, head to nod (not necessary), and eyes to turn. The face is made up with grease paint (the eyes are glass), and he is freshly made up nearly every evening. The head I am using is seventeen years old. We have been through many adventures together, so I may be forgiven if I say I love him. To me he is absolutely alive.

You must give your figures life. At first it will seem difficult to work these figures, but practice will soon enable you to overcome any bad working. Have long talks with the figures, watch them and watch yourself.

Buying your Figure.—At first, buy a cheap head for practising the movements of the levers (mouth, head and eyes). Don't pay more than about thirty-five shillings for it. Will Goldston, Ltd., will serve you admirably at that price. Practise the opening of the mouth and the nodding of the head, also the eye movement, one at a time. Rest the head by the end of the stump an a table and carry on your conversation, and practise hard. When you think you can master all the movements buy a better figure and dress it to the character you want.

Repairs.—When I first went to America, I found on my arrival at Minneapolis that my guaranteed American cabin trunk (made in I-don't-know-what-land and bought by me in the Strand) was smashed, buckled and finished. My first thoughts were of Jim (my Jim was just as important as myself). When I found him his poor little face was smashed into pulp and I was due on the stage in two hours. I begged from my wife her gloves (those nice long white kid gloves); I also asked her to hold the stage until I was ready. I then told " Mac " (my chum who helped me in my sketch), to rush out and get some seccotine and tacks.

Off came my coat and waistcoat and, locking my dressing-room against all intrusion, I started to " fake-up " Jim; but where to start, and how, was the thing. The neck was fractured, the head horribly mutilated, and one of the glass eyes smashed into small pieces. First I put the eye together with the aid of a match box and cotton wool, so that the wood base of the eye was held in position. Then, piece by piece, the glass eye was fixed into place and left for the seccotine to dry. With the aid of a cigar box I fixed the forehead to the back of the neck (cutting the wood to the shape) and then, after making a good solid job of it I covered the face with seccotine and placed linen all over it (cutting it to fit). Then I seccotined again, covering the face with kid from the glove (time, one hour). Next, I built up and padded the head with

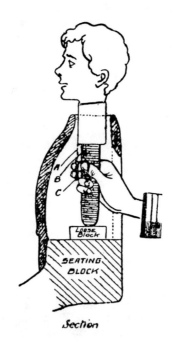

Section

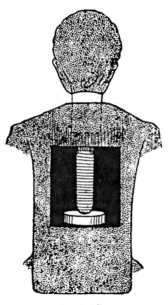

Back View

tissue paper and linen, tacked these down, and replaced the wig.

The last thing to do was to make " Jim " up. He had lost his eyelashes and eyebrows which were made of real hair, so they had to be marked in with " black " eyebrow pencil. At last he was finished in one hour and three-quarters, and in another twenty minutes he and I were making our bow to a new audience, and I think I may be forgiven if I say that for once in my life I felt nervous.

Since that mishap I do all the repairs necessary to the figure myself, and my object in telling this little experience of mine is to advise my readers also to be their own repairers. But you must thoroughly understand the mechanism of the figure. Strip it of the working parts, so as to see the movements of the springs, etc.

By removing the wig the back part of the head can be opened and everything mechanical seen.

Ball Movement for Figures.—This is a very excellent movement for working figures at a distance, such as invalid in chair, dog, figure on the horse, etc. The ball is of rubber piping (baby's bottle tubing size), and at the other end is a small flat rubber bladder. On the ball being pressed the bladder pushes up the lever which opens the mouth (see plate). The head is turned from side to side by strings fixed to a metal pin (see fig.). But if you want natural movement you must use the lever. With the ball movement the head does not move naturally.

This does not, however, matter in the case of the invalid figure, which, through illness of course, is slow and awkward in its movements.

CHAPTER XI.

Here is a little dialogue which may help you with your practice while you are alone with your figure.

(Ventriloquist entering room in the morning).

CHARACTERS.

Victor (Ventriloquist); **Fred** (Figure).

V. Hello, Fred, how are you ?

F. Good morning, Victor; I am feeling fine.

V. No, that won't do, Fred, my boy, you are not looking at me.

F. Try again.

V. That's better; but you opened your mouth too much.

F. Well, balance the lever better. Of course I must open my mouth wider for some words, also to get inflexion.

V. That's it, Fred; we want inflexion.

F. Don't you think my neck is out of my collar too far ?

V. Quite right; but my hands feel cramped.

F. That means you are not comfortable; " get comfy." (**Here Victor will see if the figure requires another square of wood under**

the " stump," or perhaps the stump wants shortening).

V. I think that's better, Fred.

F. No ! I don't like that nasty click with my mouth. Prince's " Jim " doesn't do it. **(On pronouncing " Prince " pay strict attention to the P; see notes on this in chapter on P, M, B, etc.)**   I think you let the lever go too quickly.

V. Right O !   I'll try again.

F. Certainly, as many times as you like.

V. No, Fred; it is not my fault.   The spring which pulls the mouth is too strong. **(Ease mouth spring.)**

F. That's much better; but there is still a click.

V. Yes, I heard it.   Perhaps if I put in a tiny strip of kid from an old glove and stick it neatly with seccotine that may obviate matters.   **(Does so.)**

F. Is that better ?

V. Yes, that's great.

F. Look here, Victor; work the mouth with the first finger and the head and eyes with the second finger.

V. I can't.   There are three levers.

F. Well, take the " eye " lever away and tie a ring on it instead, put the second finger through the ring and rest it on the head lever.   **(Victor does so.)**

V. I can't get you to work properly, Fred.

F. Take a rest.   Practise your voice and improve your imagination.   Why, you have only just got me, and if we are to be friends we must know each other well.

V. You are right, Fred ! Good morning.

F. Good morning. I'm here when you want me

(CURTAIN. **That is to say, take the head out of the socket and Fred then becomes a figure.**)

If you work more than one figure, practise first the figure you work with your left hand. It must never be worked with the right, and vice versa. The levers of the left hand figure must, of course, be opposite those of the right hand one. If you use the " ball " lever (see previous chapter) you can run the tubing anywhere, but I strongly advise the close working of figures (with lever). You can work the neck movement more naturally. The neck movement is done by the way you hold the stump. Care must be taken that you move only the forearm and the wrist, holding the stump just clear of the " stand." The stump is held between the thumb, third finger and little finger. When the figure speaks to you, turn the head slowly, and the eyes move around at the same time. (It is only necessary to have the eyes to turn to the left if the figure is worked by the right hand, and **vice versa** for the left).

I have just added to my figure eyes which perpetually look to the left, but with a slight strain on the eye string they look forward. A stronger pull causes them to look to the right.

Notice your own movements, such as that indicating surprise (a quick turn of the head with a slight throw back), also the eyes when soliloquizing (the head slightly droops and looks away to the half right).

All kinds of exclamations, both bright and pathetic, are made by the slight backward throw of the head or the forward droop.

The backward throw is done by pushing the " stump " forward, and this is regulated by yourself. The quick throwback is done by the quick forward push. When working the figure be very careful not to open the lips very wide. This is a big mistake made by lots of ventriloquists. Another great mistake sometimes made by ventriloquists is seen when, in playing the part of a non-commissioned officer, they insist on playing the officer. In conversation the most uneducated in the audience can detect the common vein which would be undetected if the character were that of a sergeant. By playing the officer they often exaggerate some point which is quite out of the picture.

Be yourself. Don't play a character above your capabilities and let the figures follow suit. Also, remember you are a public orator. A command of the King's English is absolutely necessary " ON " if you don't possess it " OFF " the stage.

Smoking and Drinking.—The cigarette, cigar or pipe can be held between the lips and balanced by the top front teeth. This can be done after a little practice, while the figure is continually speaking, providing you do not move the muscles of the lips. Of course, while you are speaking in your natural voice and moving the lips, the cigar or whatever you are smoking (a cigarette is the lightest, but the smoke gets into your eyes) will wobble about, but there should not be the slightest movement or wobble while the figure is talking.

SMOKING

DRINKING

To drink during a performance is harder, as you have to speak in between the drinks, and you must on no account breathe while the glass is at the lips or air will cover the glass and the voice will be muffled.   Rest the glass on the bottom lip, hold the bottom jaw stiffly, let the top lip rest very slightly on the glass.   Take short sips, one—two—three—(swallowing at the same time). Figure speaks here. Don't move glass away from mouth while figure is speaking, but only when you wish to laugh or speak yourself, and don't forget to hold your breath and speak softly, slowly and clearly, cutting the ends of the words sharply.

I do not expect you to do this at once. It was done by me at first quite accidentally, and it went so well that I kept it in the act and am always improving on it.

CHAPTER XII.

Perhaps the reader may now feel inclined to say, "And when I have done all this—read and understand, practised hard and am ready—how can I get work?"

Nearly every manager will give you a trial, if you approach him properly. Write to the manager, enclosing a stamped envelope for reply, and briefly state your business. Remember they are busy men, and have your letter typewritten so that they may read it quickly. Don't just try one manager but many, or a letter to several good agents will answer the purpose. I should prefer to write to a manager direct. At present the field is large and managers are always looking out for original ventriloquial artists.

But before trying for public work you should test your abilities before private audiences.

Have a few friends in and give them a show. It will help the student to feel what it is like to perform before real people, and he is positively sure of getting direct criticism. His friends will quickly pick out his defects; and although he will be annoyed at first, later on, when he has remedied these defects, he will thank them. He should not take the remarks too seriously to heart, but listen to all and then work harder. The next time the student gives a show his friends will see he has improved and will tell him so.

When he feels equal to the task the student may benefit by performing with a Concert Party, or an Entertainment Company, or at the seaside. This means hard work, but that is what the beginner wants. Most of the managers connected with these entertainments will let you do a show. Incidentally, I may say that I myself started in this way. Agents who book for variety theatres are all over London and the provinces, and if the beginner has paid strict attention to this book and practised hard, he will be good enough for these agents to book him.

Performing in a Room.—When you are performing in a room, be natural. Don't stare, don't keep looking at the front row, but just at your own height. Don't be nervous because so many people are confronting you. It is a test of self-confidence, and you must be equal to it. Don't shout or strain; talk softly; it is easier.

The modern ventriloquist should refrain, as far as possible, from working his figure

E

on his knee.   If there is a grand piano in the room, put the figure on the lid while you lounge by his side in the " bend," or put him on the arm of your chair.   Get your figure as close as you can without being too familiarly close.   The distance from your audience should be about six to seven feet, and all light should be at front of you.

For Stage Work.—The voice is louder (though not too loud).   Speak precisely and a little slower than in a room, and get inflexion into your voice.   The beginner should see as many ventriloquial acts as possible, so as to see what to do and what not to do.

Imagination.—Imagination plays a most important part in the ventriloquist's life. He must not only imagine, but must live the part he is playing.   He must also believe that his figure is ALIVE, and that the character played by the figure is played by him (the figure) and not the ventriloquist. Whatever you do, cultivate IMAGINATION.

An Actor.—The ventriloquist must be an actor.   His lines should be spoken correctly and not " gobbled."   His voice (if harsh), must be modulated; his enuniciation must be clear and not loud; he must carry a certain amount of dignity according to the part he is playing.   The correct mannerisms for his part and that of his figure must be studied. The ventriloquist must also understand the meaning of every word he utters.

Jokes.—It is good practice to play little ventriloquial jokes on your friends.   Here are two of my own that come to my recollection as I write.

It was in the summer, and my wife and myself had been dining with friends. After dinner we played cards, and later it began to get a bit cold, so my friend's wife said, " Gene, close the doors (French windows leading to the garden) and bolt them for the night." My friend rose, closed the window, pulled the shutters around, and the bar across. Just as he had finished I thought I would try a joke, so imitated a cat meowing faintly. My friend's wife cried, " Oh, Gene! the cat's outside." " Let him stop there," said Gene. " Oh listen to the poor thing; open the door and let him in." " Hang the cat!" said Gene. I am not certain about the word " hang." Anyhow, he opened the window and called, " Puss! Puss! Puss!" The thrice-called puss came out from **under the table.**

" Why, here's the—— " Just then he caught sight of me busily reading and—— Well, he's a much bigger man than I am, so I took refuge in flight; in fact, evaporated. I had made him open the window again, and to this day he tells the story as a huge joke against himself.

The other one I have played several times with great success. I produce a basket with two " spring " snakes in it. Then I mimic the cry of a puppy and, of course, the people want to see the " dear little thing." I tell them not to open the basket, as the puppy is rather ferocious and likely to jump at them. " But it is only a wee puppy," they say; " do let's have a look at him." Then someone opens the basket and out spring the snakes. A scream is heard and——

Well, if you do it, get near the door; be a good runner, and don't come back for half-an-hour. Then you will get your laugh.

CHAPTER XIII.

Here is a dialogue which may be useful to the beginner at figure work. It is worked with a little girl figure, nicely dressed.

" Cop."

Idea: Young gentleman (Christopher Heneker or ventriloquist's own name) is shown into drawing-room, to await his fiancée. Sitting on arm of chair is a little " girl " reading a toy book (figure).

SERVANT (**opening door and showing in** CHRISTOPHER). Will you please take a chair, sir. Mrs. Weston is out, but Miss Weston will be in in about a quarter-of-an-hour. (**Sees** KATHLEEN (the figure) **sitting on arm of chair**). Will you come to the nursery, Miss Kathleen.

KATHLEEN. No, Miss Kat'leen stay here.

CHISTOPHER. Please allow her to remain; she will be company for me, and I like babies.

SERVANT. Very well, sir. (**Exit.**) (CHRIS. **sits down on armchair.**)

CHRIS. (**to** KATHLEEN). And how are you, little one?

KATH. Ain't little one, an' I ain't a baby. I's a big girl; say you're sorry.

CHRIS. I am very sorry, I humbly apologise.

KATH. What's that 'pologise?

CHRIS. That means I beg your pardon.

KATH. Nanny says, " Say you are sorry, or stand in the corner, you little debbil." Is you a little debbil?

CHRIS. I hope not, dear—where's your Nanny now?

KATH. In the garden, looking for me. (**Laughs.**) Who is you ?

CHRIS. I have called to see your sister, Nellie.

KATH. Is you soljer man?

CHRIS.   No, I'm not a soldier.

KATH.   Is you Cop?

CHRIS.   Cop?   Whose Cop?

KATH.   Nellie told mamma she'd got a fine Cop.

CHRIS.   Is Cop a dog?

KATH.   No, Cop's Cop ; dog's Pete (**name of their dog**).

CHRIS.   Tell me about Cop.

KATH.   Nellie went to the Horses Show, and when she came home mamma said, " Was it good?" and Nellie said, " Fine; I've got a capture——"

CHRIS.   Capture?

KATH.   Yes, and he's got money—he's a great Cop for me; does Cops have chochies as well as money?

CHRIS.   Why, dear?

KATH.   'Cos Nellie brought home lots and lots of chochies——

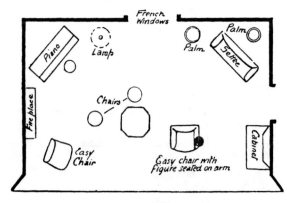

DRAWING   ROOM

CHRIS. What else did she say about the "Cops?"

KATH. She said Cop was better than the Captain—I like soljer captains, do you?

CHRIS. Y-e-s.

KATH. And she has other soljer men, and she's got a sailor man too, and lots of chochies, and rings—and—a umbrella—and——

CHRIS. What did she say about the Cop?

KATH. He is coming Tuesday—and the others have got to be " put off." What's put off?"

CHRIS. Oh! laid aside.

KATH. What's Toosday?

CHRIS. This is Tuesday.

KATH. Oh! Then you are the Cop?

CHRIS. I suppose I must be. (**Looks at watch.**) She is due in about four minutes.

KATH. What's four minutes?

CHRIS. Nothing, dear; tell Nellie I have just gone to get you some chocolates.

KATH. Big ones ?

CHRIS. Yes, dear, and I will send you them by post. (**Walk to door.**) Good-bye, dear big girl.

KATH. Good-bye, " Cop."
(**Exit.**)

(The last good-bye of KATHLEEN **can be worked by hand of assistant, who also takes part of servant through screen.)**

NOTE.—This dialogue can be varied or added to according to the wit of the performer. Any childish gags, so long as you keep to the plot, will do.

CHAPTER XIV.

The following little dialogue is for page and footman, and the scene is laid in the library (the footman is the ventriloquist and the page is the figure), William (footman), Teddie (page). Teddie discovered sitting on edge of table reading sporting paper. Enter William, goes to sideboard, pours himself out whisky and soda.

WILLIAM (**walks over to table, puts drink down, lights cigar, sits on chair near** TEDDIE). Hullo, Teddie, me boy, what's the Pioneer marked off ?

TEDDIE. Long shot for the two-thirty; two lines underneath it. That means it's a " job," don't it?

Will. ' Sure thing." Go on; read up.

TED (**reading**). He's marked "Evensedy" for the three o'clock. Two crosses, that means follow it.

WILL (**looking over** TEDDIE'S **shoulder**). We dropped a lump on that when she ran last time, so let's do the usual. I see he marks Security for the three thirty, and another " job " for the four o'clock.

TED (**drops paper, and looks at** WILLIAM). We look like having a good day, Willie, me boy.

WILL. Sure thing.

TED. Who was the girl he had in for tea yesterday?

WILL. Actress—wasn't she a picture?

TED. Yes; but a grease paint and powdered picture. Did you get the black on her eyes? And she smelt like the air smells in the " Sweet Pea " Garden; she wasn't a' actress.

WILL. How do you know?

TED. Metallurgique car. Paquin frock. Picture hat. Silk stockings, "flesh 'uns," showing through slip of skirt. Actresses don't wear those things.

WILL. No?

TED. No. Too conspicvious. 'Sides, she hadn't a dog.

WILL. Lummy, you are a " one," Ted; you do weigh 'em up; wish I'd been a scout.

TED. All right; shut up; let that go.

WILL. Do you think he will marry her ?

TED. Not Pymalion likely.

WILL. Ain't he hot stuff?

TED. Yes; but he's a worker too. Look at that big bear he shot in Africa.

WILL. Sure it was Africa?

TED. Something like it.

WILL. Ted, I thought that thing moved last night.

TED. Too much drink.

WILL. Listen; I was going upstairs.

TED. Usual way.

WILL. No. Walking.

TED. Early?

WILL. 4.30 a.m. after he came home.

TED. Oh; you'd slept it off.

WILL. Chuck it.

TED. It's chucked. Go on with the tragic description of your ascension of the moving staircase.

WILL. Right; just as I got to the top—
you know that thing stands just by the bal-
ustrade?

TED. Yes.

WILL. Well; he seemed to turn towards
me and opened his mouth and said—

TED. Brother.

WILL. No.

TED. Perhaps he thought you were his
sister.

WILL. No; he said a low growl—
" Ough " like that.

TED. Do it again.

WILL. Ough.

TED. That's like a baby crocodile ask-
ing its mother for milk.

WILL. You can't be serious, can you? Have you dusted all around and put his letters away?

TED. Yes, including the one he was determined to answer this morning.

WILL. Didn't he answer it?

TED. No, nor will he, unless dear mamma comes up on a visit; he's always good for twenty-four hours then.

WILL. I wonder where he'd be if it wasn't for us; he never knows what coloured ties and socks he should wear.

TED. You wouldn't know if you didn't read the divorce news and take stock of the " clobber " the " Co " wears.

WILL. You know, Ted; you will look quite aristocratic when I have pushed that nose of your's into your face.

TED. And you will lose your shop if I explain to him how the silk skirts and loose change disappear.

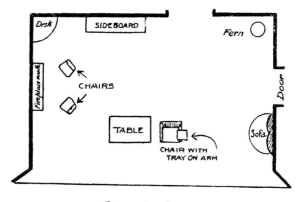

DINING   ROOM

WILL. And what would the governor do then, poor thing?

TED. If you did half what I do for him you'd **do**.

WILL. What do you do?

TED. Don't I know 'em all? (**Imitating**). No, miss; Mr. Lodes is not at home. Important business with his solicitor about his new book.

WILL. What book?

TED. Swank; Willie, me boy, all this time he's lunching with that bounder " Bottles " and the gang and kicking up " Old Harry " in the billiard room. Remember the afternoon his Uncle Jim came?

WILL. That was a near shave.

TED. I said he'd gone to his club.

WILL. Yes, and he had only just come in and was getting forty winks.

TED. And the old man said, " Whose that snoring?"

WILL. Yes; and you said we had the painters in the study, and one of them was asthmatic.

TED. I didn't want him to see the guvernor in evening dress in the afternoon. I said we were having spring cleaning and the old man said, " What! in August?"

WILL. And you said that we spring cleaned four times a year.

TED. Well, we do help him out! Don't we?

WILL. Not half, he looked fine when the sun shone on him this morning.

TED. Did you hear him say, " What are you doing there, you imp?"

WILL. Yes; what were you doing? I had to run up for another pair of gloves for him and I didn't hear.

TED. I said, "Nothing, sir; only wiping my boots on the income tax paper so you shan't read who it's sent to."

WILL. Oh! is that why he said " Good boy? "

TED. That was it! and oh, Willie, isn't that his new matchbox on the mantelpiece.?

WILL. Dash ! so it is. I've sent him out without matches, and he is calling on the girl who gave it to him.

TED. Give it to me, I'll run to the club. He is sure to drop in for his morning "pint," and I'll do the horses as I come back. (WILLIAM **gets the matchbox, saying aloud as he goes for it**)—

WILL. There'll be trouble if he doesn't get it.

TED. For you.

WILL. Go on; off you go, Teddie, my boy. (**Lifts** TEDDIE **up by the bent arms (elbows) at back and pretends to half carry and push him to door, shouts after him**). Don't forget to do a double.

TED (**in distance**). All right. (**Street door bell rings.**)

WILL. See who that is.

TED (**in distance**). (**Distant voice.**) All right (**as though speaking to somebody at**

door). No, Lady Glory; he is not in. (**Door bangs.**)

WILL. Ted (**shouts**), Teddie ! (**Listens and then looks at the audience.**)

CURTAIN.

CHAPTER XV.

The idea of the following sketch is the introduction of different nationalities into a ventriloquial performance. The figures could be human beings surmounted with ventriloquial head and shoulders.

SCENE.—The Smoking-room at a Cosmopolitan Club.

CHARACTERS.

Jack Smart	Ventriloquist
Pat, Sandy, Llewellen, Van Dunk,	
Le Grand, Silas . . .	All Figures.

JACK (to VAN DUNK). Well, I thought some of the fellows would be up by now, Van!

VAN DUNK (**who is sitting in arm chair**). Ja! mine friendt they will pe along in the minute, think you so?

JACK. Yes! I want to see them before we go off.

PAT. Hullo (**enter PAT**) Jack, me old buck, put it there; glad to see you. (**They shake hands**).

JACK. Glad to see you Pat.

.

PAT. I want to introduce you to a pal of mine, Silas Quimby; a real American and quite entitled to be one of the Pioneers.

VAN DUNK. I know Patrick. I did meet him in der Philistines, I mean Philippine's.

PAT. Well, dear old Van, glad you could get here to-night. How is it with you?

VAN DUNK. Der same, goot friendt, all goot.

JACK. Here is your friend, Pat——

(Enter SILAS QUIMBY.)

Hello! Si—how are you? Pat here wants to introduce you to me.

SILAS. Say! by the jumping jimmey! if it ain't Jack Smart. Howdy? and old Van Dunk—Gee! we only want Sandy and Llewellen here and we have the bunch of the gang.

PAT. Sure they will be here in a tick.

VAN DUNK. If dat Scotchman argues with me to-night I'll push him in der face——

SILAS. Gee! You two do go at it, it's worse than me and Le Grand; he will always speak French when I don't understand him. Gee! he rattles along like a subway express.

JACK. Do they rattle, Si?

SILAS. You ought to know; you helped to build it.

(Enter LE GRAND and LLEWELLEN.)

LE GRAND. Ah: mes enfants comment allez vouz?

SILAS. Fine; how's yourself?

LE GRAND. Trés bien. Merci.

LLEW. How are you everybody?

VAN DUNK. We are all here and now we listen to our friendt Jack.

JACK. Comrades!

SILAS. Here! Here!

PAT. Hurrah!

(**Enter** SANDY.)

SANDY. Wait for me, mon! Would ye speak without Scotland listening?

PAT. I'm listening for ye, me Scottish laird.

SANDY. Deed, mon! if there isn't my friend Van Dunk.

VAN DUNK. I will not drink her visky until Jack is finished.

SANDY. And afterwards?

LE GRAND. Vee will, mon ami.

SILAS. You bet yer! na good " high ball " for mine; what say you, Llewellen?

LLEW. I will not say on whateffer.

JACK. Boys! There's room for a railroad through the desert of the South of Sahara, and I've got the job. Or, better still, we have got the job. Sandy and Le Grand will look on and fix the road. Van Dunk will do the minerals. Paddy will see to the labour and get the managing into order. Llewellen will attend to the doctoring department. I have the plans all in order, and will see to the office department. Each man will look after his own guns and ammunition as usual, for I expect a little trouble before we get through. Now that's the propersition; are you all **on**?

SILAS. Haven't I got a job?

JACK. Didn't I say we expected trouble?

SILAS. Sure.

JACK. Well, my old scout, that's where you come in; and there's the transportation and contracting to do. I help you a little with that.

SILAS. I'm on.

LE GRAND. Moi aussi!

SANDY. I'll also sign on.

VAN DUNK. Ja! me too.

PADDY. Sure we are all with ye, Jack, me boy!

JACK. Thanks, boys.

SANDY. Here's wishing every success to the venture, mon! We are seven, and long may we continue so!

LE GRAND. Bien! here! here! I drink—

PAT (**interrupting**). Not yet, Le Grand.

LLEW. Le Grand means he drinks in spirit——

SILAS. Not of spirit.

JACK. That comes later.

VAN DUNK. And den that Scotchman he goes mad——

SANDY. Shut up, you Dutchman, and come and drink and smoke——

JACK. Yes! let's drink to the health of the Pioneers.

SILAS. And our Cosmopolitan Club.

LE GRAND. And our toast is to be?

PAT. " To all good Scouts."

F

CHAPTER XVI.

The following is another sketch for several characters.

MRS. BROWN'S TEA PARTY.

CHARACTERS.

'Arry (a Coster) . . . Figure.
Bill (a Hawker) . . . Figure.
Mrs. Noss (a Charwoman) . Figure.
Mrs. Soda (a Washerwoman) . Figure.
Mrs. Brown . . . . The Ventriloquist.

SCENE.—Mrs. Brown's parlour at 4.43 p.m. 'Arry, Mrs. Noss and Mrs. Brown having tea.

Curtain rises and Mrs. Brown is discovered sitting between 'Arry and Mrs. Noss. These figures can be worked by ball movement, the heads to turn by the lever, or cup and ball movement.

MRS. BROWN. Well ! it's as I was a-saying, Mrs. Noss, says I, to 'Arry here. It being my birthday, I think a little cup of tea (with something short in it) to my dear friends (meaning you, Mrs. Noss, and 'Arry here) would be just the thing, seeing as our 'Arry here is busy all morning, and you the same, so I gets some nice cold 'am and 'ere we are——

'ARRY. Mrs. B., I give you " many 'appy returns," and old mother Noss here——

MRS. NOSS. 'Arry ! who you talking to ?

'ARRY. Begging your pardon, Mrs. Noss—— It's a phrase of endearingness for you, showing 'ow I think of you. And you, Mrs. B., may you live long enough to er—to——

MRS. B. I know what you mean, 'Arry, and I likes you for saying it.

MRS. N. Saying what ?

MRS. B. Ah ! I know 'Arry, he's a sympathetic 'eart 'as 'Arry.

MRS. N. 'As he ?

MRS. B. 'E 'as !

'ARRY. You bet yer ! I brought yer some of those nice " taters " along, and a bit of greens and things for your birthday. They're over there in that sack. What's ye crying for, Mother—er Mrs. Noss.

MRS. N. I was a thinking of my poor old man, he used to talk like you 'Arry.

'ARRY. 'Ow long 'as he been dead ?

MRS. N. Fifteen years.

'ARRY. And you can still remember him ? " Bli-me," you 'ave got a " think-box."

MRS. N. When you gets married, 'Arry, and you die, your wife will think of you thirty years after——

'ARRY. 'Ere chuck it !——

MRS. N. Yes, it's the kindness we always feel——

'ARRY. And the smacks in the jaw ?

MRS. N. My Noss never raised 'is 'and to me once.

MRS. B. No ! that he never did, 'Arry.

'ARRY. Wasn't he the " armless sailor '
who used to play the organ ?

MRS. N. Yes !

'ARRY. Now I understand.

MRS. N. 'Ere comes Mrs. Soda down the
street——

MRS. B. I don't like that woman, and I
bet Bill the 'Awker ain't far off.

(MRS. SODA **comes to door with bundle of
washing in her arms.**)

MRS. SODA. Good evening, Mrs. Brown.
I wishes you a many 'appy return of the day.
I would come in to your party only as you
did not ask me I won't. Still I know my
manners well enough to wish you many
'appy returns.

(MRS. SODA **walks off, passing window.**)

MRS. N. The sour-tempered thing.

'ARRY. She's 'ot !

MRS. B. I don't like her, she puts
" chloridy " lime in the washing, and that
ain't quite the thing.

MRS. N. And 'ere comes Bill——

'ARRY. Scandal in 'igh life—I will 'ave
to write a letter to **John Bull** about it.

(BILL **comes up to door with his pack under
his arm.**)

BILL. What cheer, 'Arry ? Wish you
many 'appy returns of the day, Mrs. Brown.
I would come in only Mrs. Soda—Lizzie that
is——

MRS. N. (**interrupting**). Lizzie !

BILL. Yus ! We're going to get fixed up, she and I. Well ! ta-ta people. See you at the club to-night, 'Arry ?

'ARRY. Right O !

(Exit BILL past window.)

MRS. B. Well, did you ever ?

MRS. N. Never ! That's what's being going on and I never suspected it.

'ARRY. Poor Bill. I thought he was sweet on you, Mrs. Noss——

MRS. N. Well, I like that, and let me tell you, 'Arry 'Awkins, if Bill 'ad asked me, I would 'ave said " no."

'ARRY. Never mind, ol' gal, and let me tell yer if Jimmie the Tailor don't ask you, you, you ask 'im.

MRS. B. Now ! 'Arry, stop yer joking.

'ARRY. 'Oow old are you, Mrs. Brown ?

MRS. B. Let me see, I was married at twenty-one, and six months after you brought 'im 'ome after he was runned over. Then 'e died, in spite of all we could do for 'im—you and me.

'ARRY. Yus. My old pal Jack—that's three years ago, ain't it ?

MRS. B. Yes, 'Arry.

MRS. N. Well, I think I will be going now.

'ARRY. No, don't go, Mrs. Noss. (To MRS. BROWN) Emma, you're about twenty-five and I'm thirty-three (MRS. BROWN gets up and places her hand over HARRY'S mouth as though to stop him speaking, and in doing

so lifts him to his feet. This must look as though Harry has got up from the chair himself.)

MRS. B.   Don't give my age away, 'Arry.

'ARRY.   Emma, will you marry me ?   I 'ave always loved you, only you preferred Jack, and you were quite right—he was the best of us two.   Will yer ?   Emmie dear ?

MRS. N.   Go on, Emma, say yes !   I know you two are in love with one another.

MRS. B.   All right, 'Arry, when ?

'ARRY.   On Sunday.   I've got a special licence.

MRS. B.   Do you mean——

MRS. N.   (**interrupting**).   No, he don't mean nothing, I made 'im do it.   Give her a kiss, 'Arry, and I think I will ask Jim the Tailor.

'ARRY (**looking at** MRS. NOSS).   He told me he hoped you would, he's so shy.

NOTE.—This sketch might well finish with a trio between 'Arry, Mrs. Brown and Mrs. Noss.

Jim.

Instructions for Working
the
Miniature Ventriloquial Figures

PLACE the figure on the right hand and slip the thumb into the little ring at the back of the figure.

Sit down in front of a looking-glass and carefully watch the reflection of your face in the glass. In order to create a perfect illusion you must practise talking without moving your lips, and at the same time you must talk in a voice which is different from your own natural voice.

The movements of the figure must be carefully studied. If the figure is supposed to be talking to you its head should be moved slightly so that it is looking towards you. When the figure is talking in an " aside " to the audience the figure should face the audience.

The most difficult words for the ventriloquist are those beginning with b, p, f, v, b, m. To overcome the difficulty, practise until satisfied such words are perfect to yourself. Sometimes the ventriloquist can shift his position in a natural manner while the figure is saying one of these difficult words and can thus disguise the lip movement.

If you know anyone with a peculiar voice which you have learned to imitate, by all means use that voice for the figure. The voice which the ventriloquist finds is easiest

for him will be the best voice for him to cultivate. Having decided on the voice, keep to
it, and do not be persuaded to change.

Keep the figure moving slightly all the
time. No one is motionless when talking.

After a little preliminary practice before
a looking-glass, learn a good dialogue and
then practise the dialogue with the figure.
Practise very slowly at first and then
gradually increase the speed until the
dialogue can be recited as though it was a
real conversation between yourself and
another living person.

When you have carried out this practice
to your own satisfaction go through a
rehearsal or two away from the glass in order
to accustom yourself to the conditions under
which you will be giving the entertainment
to your friends. Go back to the glass again
and watch for any movements of your lips
and facial muscles. If the mouth is opened
slightly, as though you were about to smile,
and the upper teeth are resting lightly on
the lower lip, you will find it an easy matter
to talk without moving your lips.

There are sure to be a few slips at the first
few performances, but you may rest assured
that the audience will not notice them if you
are managing the figure properly. All eyes
are on the figure during a ventriloquial
performance, and if the dialogue is smart
and amusing and the figure moves in a lifelike manner the audience will be thoroughly
well entertained. Learn to regard the figure
as though it was a living being, and the
audience will regard it in the same way and
you will obtain just the effect which the
ventriloquist always wishes to produce.

The mouth of the figure must move as the mouth of a living person would move if that person was saying the words which, apparently, come from the figure.

Practise—**practise**—PRACTISE, and remember that three-fourths of the illusion of the talking figure is provided by the figure itself.   Make it as lifelike as possible.   Look at the figure when you are talking to it, and at the audience when you are speaking to the audience.   But, when all is said and done, the only way to become a ventriloquist is to PRACTISE.

Ventdollie Dialogue
for Boy and Girl Figures

V.: Well, little fellow, how are you ?

B.: I am not a little fellow; I am a man.

V.: Why, not already, surely ?

B.: That is part of me.

V.: What do you mean ? Part of you ?

B.: I am a man-in-kin.

V.: Manikin !

B.: Man ye-ken—Scotch?—joke—ha, ha!

V.: Of course, you go to school ?

B.: Yes, but it's forced upon me.

V.: Don't you like school ?

B.: Don't ask silly questions; is there a boy who likes school ?

V.: Well, we all liked school.

B.: That's what you grown-ups say— when you have left.

V.: I would like to go back to school.

B.: Well, go back for me.

V.: School is a most wonderful place; it's the foundation of your career.

B.: Career !

V.: You know what career means ?

B.: Yes !

V.: What does it mean ?

B.: He's a poor man who takes the rich round the world.

V.: No, that's a courier—I said career.

B.: Oh, a career is what couriers are when they make their career as a courier.

V.: Very nicely put.   Tell me, how do you get on with arithmetic ?

B.: I don't get on, that's where I get off.

V.: But, it's quite simple—what sums do you do ?

B.: I do a lot, but they are never right.

V.: Well, here's a short one for you. Suppose your father owed me five sovereigns last September and he paid me back one sovereign every month; how much would he owe me in January ?

B.: Five sovereigns.

V.: You don't know what I mean.

B.: You don't know father.

V.: Well, what you lose at arithmetic you make up at repartee.   Can you spell very well ?

B.: V-E-R-Y—W-E-L-L.

V.: Good !

V.: Can you spell Russia ?

B.: That's where the red serviettes come from.

V.: No.   Soviet, not serviette.

B.: I always thought it was serviettes.

V.: Well, can you spell Russia ?

B.: Yes !

V.: Well, spell it.

B.: I-T.

V.: No, Russia.

B.: N O R U S H E R.

V.: Oh ! No, no, no—that's wrong.

B.: Well, you spell Russia.

V.: R U S S I A,

B.: I thought you meant a lady—RUSH-ER, or even that's wrong, 'cause it's " her " —RUSH-HER.

V.: How old are you ?

B.: Nine. I should have been ten had Daddy met Mother a year before—at least, that's what Uncle Bill says.

V.: Oh ! you have an Uncle Bill ?

B.: Who hasn't an Uncle Bill ?

V.: Is your Uncle Bill a nice man ?

B.: Very nice—always 2s. 6d. when he comes.

V.: Was that your Uncle Bill I met at lunch yesterday—the fat man with rather a rubicand nose ?

B.: Oh ! is that the name of his nose ? Did he have a squint in his eye ?

V.: No.

B.: Did he wear riding breeches ?

V.: No !

B.: Did he scoop up his gravy with his knife ?

V.: No !

B.: Well, that's him.

V.: By the way, I noticed you were looking at him very hard—in fact, rather rudely. Why was this ?

B.: Mother says he drinks like a fish; so I watched him, as I wanted to see how a fish drank.

V.: I suppose your Uncle Bill is a great traveller?

B.: Yes ! Been all over the world.

V.: How many times has he crossed the Equator ?

B.: Crossed the Equator ?

V.: Why, every schoolboy knows what the Equator is.

B.: Oh, yes !

V.: Do you ?

B.: Yes.

V.: Well, what is it ?

B.: I only said " Yes " to save an argument.

V.: Now what is the Equator ?   Surely, you know ?

B.: The Equator is a menagerie lion running around the earth.

V.: No, no, no—an imaginery line—line, not lion.

B.: You know what it is ?

V.: Yes, of course I do.

B.: Well, why ask me ?

V.: I was testing your knowledge.

B.: Well, why pick me out of all the millions in the world ?

V.: Tell me when do you go back to school ?

B.: Oh ! let's talk about something pleasant.

V.: Well, when do your holidays finish ?

B.: The day before we have roast chicken.

V.: Why do you say that ?

B.: 'Cause we never have roast chicken only when I go back to school.

V.: Do you have sports at your school ?

B.: Rather, and entertainments and plays. I am a piece of a quartette.

V.: Well, what part do you take ?

B.: I am not sure whether I take the " quart " or the " tette."   Might I ask you a question ?

V.: Yes.

B.: What is the thing called you see boys riding along the street with two wheels and two pedals ?

V.: A bicycle.

B.: Why is it called a bicycle ?

V.: Bi means two—the wheels,cycle, so it is bi-cycle.

B.: What's one with three wheels ?

V.: A tri-cycle.

B.: I saw a man with one wheel yesterday. What's that ?

V.: Oh, that's a uni-cycle.

B.: No, it was a wheelbarrow.

V.: So you're quite a singer ?

B.: Well, would you like to hear me sing?

V.: I certainly should.

B.: Well, you've brought it on yourself, it's sure to spoil our friendship.

FINISH WITH A SONG OR RECITATION.

V.: And what is your name, little lady ?

G.: No, it's not " little lady," it's Dorothy Deane.

V.: Oh !

G.: When Mother's pleased with me she calls me Dot, but when she is cross it's Dorothy.

V.: Oh ! I see. Do you go to school ?

G.: Yes ! But I like the Aquarium better.

V.: Aquarium ? So you went to the Aquarium, did you ?

G.: Yes !

V.: Did you see all the fishes ?

G.: Yes, but I did not see the "timmies."

V.: Didn't see what, dear ?

G.: The " Timmies." Don't you know?

V.: No; I don't.

G.: Why, it says the Lord made Heaven, earth, the sea and the " timmies."

V.: Oh ! I see you mean Heaven, earth, the sea and all that-in-them-is.

G.: I thought it were " timmies." No wonder I could not find them.

V.: So you know a little about Scripture?

G.: Oh, yes !

V.: Tell me what did David mean when he said he would rather be a doorkeeper in the House of the Lord ? Is that too much for you ?

G.: No. He means that he could walk about while the sermon is being preached.

V.: Do you know anything about geography ?

G.: Geo-gra-phy ? Yes !

V.: Can you tell me the names of the chief mountains in Scotland ?

G.: Ben Nevis, Ben Lomond, and Ben Johnson.

V.: Oh ! you know too much about geography. I must ask you something else. Suppose I had a pound of steak ?

G.: Yes !

V.: And I cut it in two. What would I have ?

G.: Halves !

V.: Now I cut them again. What do I have ?

G.: Quarters !

V.: Now I cut them again. What shall I have this time ?

G.: Eighths.

V.: And now I again cut them. What would I have ?

G.: Sixteenths.

V.: Good girl, and now I cut the monce again, and what shall I have ?

G.: Mince-meat !

V.: You are a very clever little girl. I wonder if you could tell me what the triple alliance is ?

G.: Faith, hope and charity.

V.: Oh ! no, no, no—but, never mind, do you know what a veteran is ?

G.: Yes !

V.: What is he ?

G.: A man who doctors horses.

V.: No, no; that's a veterinary surgeon. I said a veteran. Shall I tell you ?

G.: Yes !

V.: A veteran is an old soldier. Do you think you will remember that ?

G.: Yes !

V.: Well, what is a veteran ?

G.: A sol-old-ger.

V.: No, a soldier.

G.: I saw the Queen yesterday. She was with a duke—real duke and his wife.

V.: Well, dear, what would you call the wife of a duke ?

G.: Duckie.

V.: Oh ! no, no, no——

G.: Oh ! yes. It's right 'cause I heard him call her that. He said, " Look at those pretty flowers, ducky."

V.: Oh ! no. The wife of a duke is the duchess. Where did you go for your holidays ?

G.: We went to see Mount Eirvivus.

V.: You mean Mount Vesuvius.

G.: That's it.

V.: Did you notice the lava ?

G.: No !

V.: Still, you know what lava means, don't you ?

G.: Yes, it's what Daddy puts on his face to shave.

V.: No, no ! I mean that which comes out of the mouth of Mount Vesuvious and runs down the sides of the mountain.

G.: But I saw it on Daddy's face.

V.: No, that's lather. I suppose you came back on a ship ?

G.: Yes ! and it blowed and blowed and snowed.

V.: So you were caught in a blizzard ?

G.: Blizzard ?

V.: Yes, blizzard ! You know what a blizzard is—don't you ?

G.: Yes, the inside of a duck !

V.: Oh ! you mean gizzard ; I said blizzard.

G.: Oh !

V.: Now tell me, do you play in your garden a lot ?

G.: Yes !

V.: Have you noticed those little wriggly things that come through a tiny hole ?

G.: Yes !

V.: Well, what's their name ?

G.: Worm !

V.: That's right; and now tell me another little creature that wriggles through the earth and comes through another small hole.

G.: Another worm.

V.: Well, that will do, but I meant a mole.

G.: I went to the zoo and saw all the animals, elephants, giraffes, and doma-dromes. Has the camel got one hump or two ?

V.: (**pauses as though thinking**): Oh ! one hump, I think.

G.: This one had two.

V.: That must have been a dromedary.

G.: I had a ride on him all round the grounds and back to the Dromedarydrome.

V.: Did you see any zebras ?

G.: No !

V.: But you know what a zebra is, don't you ?

G.: Yes ! He is like a horse, but striped, and is used as a picture for a " Z." I went to church on Sunday.

V.: Did you ? What church do you go to ?

G.: Church of England.

V.: Can you tell me the name of the head of the Church of England ?

G.: The Archipelago of Canterbury.

V.: Can you spell ?

G.: No: but I can sing.

V.: Talking of singing, birds sing don't they ?

G.: Yes; I have got one in a bird-cage that sings.

V.: Have you ? Can you spell bird-cage ?

G.: No !

V.: Well, I'll teach you. B-I-R-D: Bird; hyphen, you know what a hyphen is, don't you ?

G.: Yes; it is what Daddy gets the soda water from for his whiskey.

V.: Oh ! no. That's a syphon.

G.: Oh !

V.: B-I-R-D — Bird; C-A-G-E — Cage — Bird-cage.

G.: Oh ! yes. I know: B-I-R-D—Bird.

V.: That's right: now a hyphen, then C-A-G-E.

G.: B-I-R-D spells bird: then hyphen and C-A-G-E spells bird hyphen cage.

V.: Oh ! no. The hyphen is only put there; do you know why the hyphen is there?

G.: Yes; it's what the bird sits on.

V.: Oh, no. That is made to join the two words together. Never mind ! you are a clever little girl. Now let me hear you sing a little song ?

———

FINISH WITH A SONG OR RECITATION.

GOLDSTON'S EXCLUSIVE FIGURE

NAUGHTY ALEC !

Cheeky Boy figure dressed in loud clothes with an expression which demands laughter on sight. Movements : Eyes, Mouth and Lip, both Arms, Head to Turn and Nod, Leg to move and Nose Lights up each time the Eye Winks. A great novelty. Price £6-10-0. Packing and Railway free in the U.K.

GOLDSTON'S SUPPLY

ILLUSIONS.

CONJURING.

JUGGLING.

VENTRILOQUIAL.

HAND SHADOWS.

BOOKS ON MAGIC

AND

KINDRED SUBJECTS.

EVERYTHING UNDER

THE HEADING OF

MAGIC AND MYSTERY

OBTAINABLE AT

GOLDSTON'S.

GOLDSTON'S BEST IS

THE WORLD'S BEST.

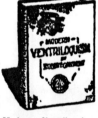

Printed in the United States
98889LV00002B/9/A